i love you

TODAY, TOMORROW & ALWAYS.

1

To My Beloved,

This book is a part of my soul, written just for you. Over the next 150 days, you'll find affirmations, poems, and words that carry the depth of my love. Each page is a moment for you to feel cherished, a daily reminder of how deeply you are loved.

Every word here is a reflection of what you mean to me— my anchor, my light, my greatest gift. As you turn each page, know that you are my everything.

"In your presence, I find peace.
In your laughter, I find joy.
In your love, I find myself."

I hope this book brings you comfort, strength, and a sense of how special you are to me. Thank you for being my partner, my love, and my forever.

Yours, always and completely,

_____

DAY #1

There's something extraordinary about the way you love me. It's not in grand gestures but in the quiet, steady ways you show you care. You are my comfort, my constant, and my greatest joy.

DAY #2

You are the kind of person who makes life brighter just by being in it. Your love feels like sunlight on a cold day— warm, reassuring, and exactly what I need.

DAY #3

You are the quiet in my chaos,
The steady rhythm when the world feels too fast.
With you, I've found not just love but peace.

DAY #4

Every moment with you feels like it's been borrowed from some dream I never thought I'd deserve. You've shown me what it means to be truly loved, and I'll never stop being grateful.

DAY #5

Being loved by you has been the greatest privilege of my life. It's not just about the good times; it's the way you stand by me in the hard moments, unwavering and true.

DAY #6

In your smile, I see my tomorrow.
In your touch, I feel my home.
In your love, I've found my reason.

DAY #7

You make the ordinary feel magical. A walk, a conversation, even the silence—all of it feels different when I'm with you. You bring beauty into everything.

DAY #8

I've loved you in ways I can't quite put into words. It's in the way my heart races when I see you and in the calm I feel when I'm near you. Loving you is my life's greatest adventure.

DAY #9

With you, I've learned that love isn't just a feeling - it's a choice we make every day. And every day, I choose you. I always will.

DAY #10

You are my light, my warmth,
The reason I believe in the good.
You are my heart's truest home.

DAY #11

There are moments when I look at you, and it feels like the universe has conspired to bring us together. You're not just my love, you are my destiny, the missing piece I didn't even know I was searching for.

DAY #12

You've become a part of me, woven so deeply into my heart that I can no longer tell where you end and I begin. Loving you isn't just something I do - it's who I am.

DAY #13

You are my every breath,
The rhythm my soul moves to.
In loving you, I've found my purpose,
My reason, my forever.

DAY #14

You've shown me a love so profound that it has redefined the way I see the world. With you, everything feels brighter, more meaningful, and infinitely more beautiful.

DAY #15

Your love has taught me that true strength lies in vulnerability, that opening my heart to you is the bravest and most fulfilling thing I've ever done. With you, I feel both fearless and safe.

DAY #16

I never believed in forever until you came into my life.

Now, forever doesn't feel like enough time

To hold you, love you, and treasure you.

DAY #17

There's a depth to my love for you that I can't fully explain. It's in every thought, every breath, and every beat of my heart. You are the centre of my universe, the reason I exist.

DAY #18

You are the first person I think of when I wake and the last before I sleep. Even in my dreams, you are there my constant, my anchor, my everything.

DAY #19

Your love is the quiet flame that keeps me warm,
A fire that never burns out,
But grows stronger with each passing day.
You are my eternal light.

DAY #20

Loving you has been the greatest transformation of my life. You've shown me what it means to truly give, to truly trust, and to truly live. With you, I've found a love that transcends words and time.

DAY #21

Loving you feels like discovering a secret part of myself I never knew existed. You've brought out the best in me, and for that, I will love you with every part of my being.

DAY #22

You are the safest place I've ever known. In your arms, the world fades, and all I feel is the unshakable certainty that I'm exactly where I'm meant to be.

DAY #23

I've loved you in a thousand little ways
In stolen glances, in quiet moments,
In the way my heart whispers your name
Even when you're not near.

DAY #24

I sometimes wonder how a single person can mean so much, and can hold so much of my heart. But then I see you, and it makes perfect sense you are everything I've ever needed.

DAY #25

You're not just the person I love, you're the person who reminds me of all the good this world has to offer. You are kindness, joy, and hope, wrapped up in the most beautiful soul.

DAY #26

With every day that passes, I find another reason to fall deeper in love with you. You are the kind of love that never grows old, never fades, only strengthens.

DAY #27

Sometimes I wonder what I did to deserve you. But then I realize that love doesn't have to be deserved it just is. And I am endlessly grateful that it's you who loves me.

DAY #28

Your love is the steady rain that nourishes my soul,

The quiet strength that helps me grow.

With you, I am whole.

DAY #29

There's a beauty in the way you love me, it's unwavering, patient, and true. It's the kind of love that changes everything, and it's made me want to be the best version of myself.

DAY #30

Every time I look at you, I feel like I'm seeing you for the first time all over again. Your presence is magic, your love is a gift, and I am endlessly in awe of you.

DAY #31

When I'm with you, I don't just feel loved I feel seen, understood, and completely accepted. You've given me the kind of love that feels like coming home.

DAY #32

Your love has changed the way I see the world. Everything feels brighter, softer, and more alive because I get to share it with you.

DAY #33

You are the calm in my storm,
The flame that keeps me warm.
In your love, I find my strength,
A bond that stretches any length.

DAY #34

Even in a room full of people, you're the only one I see. You're not just the love of my life you're the center of my universe.

DAY #35

I used to think love was a fleeting feeling, but you've shown me that it's a choice, a commitment to grow together, to lift each otherup, and to always hold on. I choose you, every time.

DAY #36

With you, I've learned that love isn't about finding someone who completes you, it's about finding someone who inspires you to complete yourself. You are my inspiration.

DAY #37

I love the way you look at the world - with kindness, curiosity, and hope. You make me want to see life through your eyes, and it's the most beautiful view.

DAY #38

If love were a journey, ours would be the most beautiful.

Through valleys and peaks, I'll walk with you,

Hand in hand, heart to heart.

DAY #39

I could search for a thousand lifetimes and still never find someone who loves the way you do. Your love is pure magic, and I am endlessly grateful for it.

DAY #40

Every part of me belongs to you. My heart, my thoughts, my dreams they all revolve around you. You are my past, my present, and every hope I have for the future.

DAY #41

Loving you has been the most natural thing I've ever done. It's like my heart knew you before I did, and every beat since has been for you.

DAY #42

You've turned my life into something extraordinary. Every moment with you feels like a treasure I never knew I was searching for but can't imagine living without.

DAY #43

You are the gentle whisper of hope on my hardest days,

The soft reminder that I'm never alone.

In your love, I've found my strength,

In your arms, my home.

DAY #44

I love the little things about you - the way your eyes light up when you smile, the way you laugh without holding back. These tiny moments remind me why you are my everything.

DAY #45

When I think about us, I don't just see love, I see partnership, trust, and a future that feels brighter than I could have imagined. With you, anything feels possible.

DAY #46

Your love has this way of healing me. It's a quiet, steady force that reminds me I'm safe, I'm valued, and I'm deeply, endlessly loved.

DAY #47

If I could write the story of my life,
Every chapter would begin with you.
You are my plot twist, my happy ending,
My everything in between.

DAY #48

There's beauty in the way you love me. It's not loud or boastful it's steady, kind, and endlessly reassuring. You've given me a love that feels like freedom.

DAY #49

With you, I've learned that love isn't just about the good times. It's about weathering the storms together, holding on, and coming out stronger on the other side. Thank you for being my rock.

DAY #50

You're not just the love of my life, you're my best friend, my greatest cheerleader, and the one person I never want to face a day without. Thank you for being my everything.

DAY #51

You have a way of making me feel like the most important person in the world, not through grand gestures but through the quiet consistency of your love. It's in the little things you do, and I notice every single one.

DAY #52

Your presence is my greatest comfort, your love my greatest treasure. I could travel the world a thousand times and never find anything as precious as the moments I spend with you.

DAY #53

Loving you is like breathing
Effortless, essential, constant.
You are the rhythm of my heart,
The very essence of my being.

DAY #54

When I'm with you, I feel a kind of peace I've never known before. It's as if all the noise in the world fades, leaving just us, two hearts beating in perfect harmony.

DAY #55

I've loved you in so many ways - quietly, passionately, deeply. And no matter how much time passes, I'll never run out of new ways to love you.

DAY #56

With you, every day feels like a new beginning. You are the spark that lights my life, the reason I wake up excited for what's ahead.

DAY #57

If love were a journey, you'd be my destination.

If love were a song, you'd be my melody.

If love were a lifetime, I'd choose you every time.

DAY #58

You've taught me that love isn't about perfection, it's about showing up, staying present, and choosing each other every single day. And every day, I choose you.

DAY #59

There's a quiet kind of magic in the way you love me. It doesn't shout or demand - it just is. And that steady, beautiful love has changed everything for me.

DAY #60

You are my favorite thought, my sweetest memory, and my greatest hope. Loving you is the most natural, most fulfilling thing I have ever known.

DAY #61

When I think of love, I think of you. Not just because of what you do, but because of who you are someone so kind, so beautiful, and so completely irreplaceable.

DAY #62

Loving you has given my life a purpose I never knew I was searching for. You've become the centre of my world, and I wouldn't have it any other way.

DAY #63

You are my heart's greatest discovery,
A love I never dreamed I'd find.
With you, my days are brighter,
And my soul is endlessly alive.

DAY #64

Your love isn't just something I feel, it's something I live. It's in every moment, every decision, every dream. You are my beginning, my middle, and my forever.

DAY #65

Being with you has taught me that love isn't about grand declarations - it's about the quiet, steady way you show up, again and again, reminding me that I am never alone.

DAY #66

With you, I've learned that love isn't perfect, but it's always worth it. Even in our flaws, even in our challenges, I find myself loving you more deeply every day.

DAY #67

Your love is a fire that warms my soul,
A light that guides my way.
In your arms, I find my courage,
And in your heart, my stay.

DAY #68

Every time I see you, I fall in love all over again. It's not just your beauty, though that takes my breath away - it's your kindness, your strength, and the way you love me without reservation.

DAY #69

You are the first person I want to share my joy with and the only one I want beside me in the hard times. Your love makes everything feel possible.

DAY #70

I didn't know it was possible to love someone this much. With every word, every touch, every glance, you make me feel like the luckiest person alive. My heart is, and will always be, yours.

DAY #71

You are the calm in my chaos, the steady hand I reach for when the world feels overwhelming. Your love has brought me peace I didn't know I was missing.

DAY #72

With you, I've learned that love isn't about perfection; it's about showing up, flaws and all, and knowing you're accepted exactly as you are. That's what you've given me - unconditional love.

DAY #73

You are my favorite moment of every day,
The thought that lingers long after night falls.
Your love isn't just part of my life- it is my life.

DAY #74

You've taught me that love isn't just a feeling it's a commitment, a promise to stand together no matter what. And I promise you, I will always stand with you.

DAY #75

When I think of us, I don't just see love, I see a partnership, a team, and a future that feels brighter because it's ours. You are my greatest adventure.

DAY #76

There are a million little ways you make my life better, from the way you laugh to the way you listen. Loving you is like discovering the world all over again.

DAY #77

Your love is the quiet strength that carries me,
The gentle reminder that I am never alone.
You are my anchor, my safe harbour.

DAY #78

I never believed in soulmates until I met you. You don't just fit into my life - you've changed it, shaped it, and made it more beautiful than I ever imagined.

DAY #79

Every day, I look at you and feel the same rush I felt the first time I saw you. It's not just love - it's awe. You are the most incredible person I've ever known.

DAY #80

You've given me a kind of love that doesn't demand or expect - it just is. It's steady, powerful, and endless. With you, I've found my forever.

DAY #81

Before you, I didn't truly understand what it meant to feel whole. You've filled the empty spaces in my heart and brought a completeness to my life I didn't know was missing.

DAY #82

You've transformed the way I see myself. Through your eyes, I've learned to be kinder to myself, to believe in my worth, and to see the beauty in who I am. That is your magic.

DAY #83

You are the shift in my story,
The turning point I didn't see coming.
Your love rewrote my life,
And every chapter since has been more beautiful.

DAY #84

With you, I've found a courage I never thought I had. You make me want to take risks, to dream bigger, and to chase the life we deserve - because I know you'll be right there with me.

DAY #85

You've taught me the true meaning of love - not just in the way you care for me, but in the way you've made me care more deeply about everything. You've awakened my heart.

DAY #86

Before you, love was just a word to me. Now it's a feeling, a promise, and a way of life. You've turned what I thought I knew about love into something so much greater.

DAY #87

Your love is the light that chased away my shadows,

The warmth that melted my fear.

You've given me the gift of living fully,

And I owe that all to you.

DAY #88

You've shown me what it means to truly be seen. With you, I don't feel like I have to hide any part of myself. You've given me the freedom to be completely and unapologetically me.

DAY #89

My life before you feels like a faded memory. You've brought colour to my world, depth to my days, and a sense of meaning I never knew was possible.

DAY #90

I didn't just fall in love with you- I found a new version of myself in your love. A stronger, happier, more hopeful me. You've changed everything, and I'll never stop being grateful.

DAY #91

You've shown me that love isn't about fixing someone - it's about growing together. With you, I've become more of myself than I ever thought possible. You make me feel complete.

DAY #92

My days used to feel so ordinary until you walked in and turned everything into magic. You've given my life colour, purpose, and a depth I never dreamed of.

DAY #93

You've taken my broken pieces,
And gently placed them back together.
Not to make me perfect,
But to make me whole.

DAY #94

Your love has been my greatest teacher. Through you, I've learned patience, vulnerability, and what it means to truly give your heart to someone. You've transformed me in ways I can't even put into words.

DAY #95

I didn't know what it was to feel truly safe until you came into my life. You've created a space for me where I can be seen, heard, and loved exactly as I am.

DAY #96

Your love didn't just enter my life - it rebuilt it. It turned my fears into courage, my doubts into belief, and my loneliness into a deep sense of belonging. You've changed me forever.

DAY #97

You are my turning point,
The moment everything shifted.
Your love made my world softer,
And my heart stronger.

DAY #98

With you, I've stopped living for the future or dwelling on the past. You've taught me to savour the present, to cherish every moment, because being with you is the greatest gift.

DAY #99

Your love has been a light in the dark corners of my soul. You've shown me beauty where I once saw flaws, and strength where I once saw weakness. You've truly changed me.

DAY #100

Before you, I was living a half-life, always searching for something I couldn't name. And then you came along and filled that space with your love. Now I know I was waiting for you all along.

DAY #101

You've taken the pieces of my life that felt scattered and uncertain, and with your love, you've turned them into something whole. I've never felt so complete.

DAY #102

With you, I've discovered a strength I didn't know I had and a happiness I didn't know was possible. You've made me believe in myself in ways no one else ever could.

DAY #103

You walked into my life like a quiet sunrise,
And before I knew it, everything was bathed in light.
Your love has awakened something in me
That I never want to lose.

DAY #104

You've taught me that love isn't about perfection - it's about showing up, choosing each other, and growing together. With you, I feel like I can face anything.

DAY #105

Before you, life felt like a puzzle with a missing piece. Then you arrived, and suddenly, everything fit. You've turned my life into something beautiful.

DAY #106

Your love has made me softer, stronger, and more alive. It's not just that you've changed my life - you've transformed the way I see myself and the world.

DAY #107

You are the heartbeat of my existence,
The quiet voice that steadies me.
With you, I've found my purpose,
And my truest self.

DAY #108

You've given me a home - not a place, but a feeling. A sense of belonging that wraps around me like the warmest embrace. I never want to let it go.

DAY #109

Loving you has changed the way I understand time. The past doesn't matter anymore, and the future feels like a gift I can't wait to open - with you by my side.

DAY #110

Your love has brought out a version of me that I didn't know existed. Someone braver, kinder, and more open. I am who I am today because of you.

DAY #111

You've made me see the beauty in the little things - the way the sunlight dances through the curtains or how a quiet moment can feel like an eternity when I'm with you. You've changed how I live, and I love you endlessly for it.

DAY #112

When I hold your hand, I don't just feel your touch - I feel your trust, your love, and your promise that no matter what, we're in this together. You are my forever.

DAY #113

In your love, I've found my truth,
A steady flame, a life renewed.
With you, my heart knows no fear,
Every day is brighter with you near.

DAY #114

You are my safe place, my heart's compass. No matter what the day brings, I know I can face it because your love is my anchor and my guide.

DAY #115

Your love has softened my edges and strengthened my soul. With you, I am both gentler and braver. You are my greatest transformation.

DAY #116

I love the way you make even the ordinary feel extraordinary. A walk, a conversation, even silence - it all feels like magic when I'm with you.

DAY #117

Your love is my quiet refuge,
A place where my heart can rest.
In you, I've found a forever,
A home within your chest.

DAY #118

You've shown me that love isn't about what you get - it's about what you give. And you give so much of yourself, so effortlessly. I'm grateful for your love every single day.

DAY #119

Every time I see you, I am reminded of why I fell in love with you. It's in the way you care, the way you laugh, and the way you simply exist with such grace.

DAY #120

You've taught me that love isn't about perfection - it's about choosing each other, over and over again. And every day, I choose you. I always will.

DAY #121

You've given me a kind of love that feels like a quiet miracle - gentle, steady, and life-changing. With you, I've found the truest version of myself.

DAY #122

You are the reason I believe in the power of love. Not because it's always easy, but because with you, it's always worth it.

DAY #123

Your love is the rhythm of my heart,
A melody that never fades.
With you, every moment feels timeless,
Every day, a song to be played.

DAY #124

You've made me see that love isn't just something we feel -
it's something we do. It's in your kindness, your patience,
and the way you show up every day for us.

DAY #125

When I'm with you, I feel like I've found the place I was always meant to be. You're not just my partner - you're my home.

DAY #126

I love the way you make me laugh, even when I don't feel like smiling. You've turned my life into something brighter, something better, just by being you.

DAY #127

You are the sunrise after my darkest night,
A constant light that guides me.
Your love is my refuge, my hope,
The reason I keep believing.

DAY #128

You've shown me that love isn't about finding someone perfect - it's about finding someone who makes you feel perfect just as you are. And that's exactly what you've done for me.

DAY #129

Every time I hear your voice, it feels like the world quiets for a moment. You are my calm in the chaos, my reason to keep going.

DAY #130

With you, I've learned that the greatest gifts in life aren't things - they're moments. The ones we share, the ones we build, and the ones that make this love so extraordinary.

DAY #131

You've turned the simple act of loving someone into the most profound experience of my life. With you, even the quiet moments feel like they hold the universe.

DAY #132

Loving you isn't just something I do - it's who I am. You've become such an inseparable part of me that I can't imagine my world without you.

DAY #133

You are the thread that weaves my days,
A quiet strength in all my ways.
Your love is my anchor, my guiding star,
No matter the distance, near or far.

DAY #134

Before you, I thought I understood love. But with you, I've learned it's not about words or gestures - it's about how you make me feel seen, cherished and understood every single day.

DAY #135

With you, I've discovered that love isn't about completing someone - it's about making them feel whole, even in their broken places. That's the gift you've given me.

DAY #136

Your love has been a quiet revolution in my life. It didn't demand or overwhelm - it simply showed up and changed everything for the better.

DAY #137

Your love is like a river,

Endless and free.

It carries me forward,

Into a life I never dreamed could be.

DAY #138

You've taught me that love doesn't have to be loud to be powerful. It's in the way you hold my hand, listen to my heart, and make me feel like I belong.

DAY #139

Every time I think of you, I feel this incredible gratitude for how you've transformed my life. You've taken an ordinary existence and turned it into something extraordinary.

DAY #140

You are the love I didn't know I needed, the partner I never dreamed I'd have, and the reason I believe the best is yet to come.

DAY #141

Loving you has been a journey of growth - together, we've learned, stretched, and become better versions of ourselves. You are my greatest lesson and my greatest reward.

DAY #142

Your love is the strength I carry with me every day. It's the quiet courage that tells me I can face anything because you're by my side.

DAY #143

You inspire me to be better, to dream bigger, and to live fuller. Your love is my motivation to reach for everything life has to offer.

DAY #144

Every day with you feels like a new adventure. Even the smallest moments with you are filled with excitement and wonder. You are my greatest journey.

DAY #145

Your love has been the balm for every wound I didn't know I was carrying. You've healed me in ways I'll never be able to thank you enough for.

DAY #146

With you, I've found a home - not a place, but a feeling of belonging. Wherever you are, that's where I want to be.

DAY #147

You've shown me parts of myself I didn't even know existed. In loving you, I've discovered a depth to life and love that I never imagined.

DAY #148

Your love has made me believe in forever. Not in a fleeting or fragile way, but in a quiet, unshakable way that feels like it's always been and always will be.

DAY #149

With you, I've found the freedom to be myself - fully and unapologetically. Your love has shown me that I don't have to change to be worthy; I just have to be.

DAY #150

You're not just my partner; you're my best friend. The one I laugh with, dream with and trust with everything. You're the one I choose, over and over.

To the One Who Holds My Heart,

As you reach the final page of this book, I hope it has been a reminder of just how deeply you are loved. Over the last 150 days, each word has been a reflection of the admiration, gratitude, and affection you inspire every day.

This book was created to celebrate the unique bond we share—a love that is steady, enduring, and filled with hope for all that lies ahead. These pages were a way to capture moments of love and appreciation, but they are only a glimpse of how much you mean.

May this book remind you, again and again, that you are cherished, valued, and loved beyond measure. The journey we share is my greatest joy, and I look forward to every moment still to come.

With love always,

_____

Printed in Great Britain
by Amazon

58022087R00088